★ ★ ★ ★ ★

I0200950

WELCOME & THANK YOU!

This multi-media book entitles you to a special gift that is the perfect companion to *Creating with the Divine.*

It is a group of videos that assist with meditation, expansion of your personal skills as well as a checklist to see what skills you may already possess and which ones you may be ready to improve.

This collection of media will allow you to study and improve your own metaphysical gifts in greater detail!

DOWNLOAD TODAY!

ThePracticalMystics.com/thanks

★ ★ ★ ★ ★

CREATING

WITH THE DIVINE

VOLUME 4 OF THE DIVINE SERIES

RENO LONGMOONS
JANINE BOLON

PRAISE FOR
CREATING WITH THE DIVINE

"This is a book of awakened spirit. So, I would clearly recommend it for anyone who is currently on or has ever been on this journey. No person can tell you to "Wake Up... or Be Awakened"; it is obviously a calling that comes from a greater source. This book, through Janine and Reno, can act as a Guide at any and maybe even All Stages of the Journey. The practical tools and teachings through story are a great asset, and by the way, I love the combination of written and audio files. There is an emotional and transformational aspect to listening to someone tell a story. I truly enjoyed the experiencing of this book. I appreciate you!"

-Mark Siegel, Personal Mind Trainer
New York Institute of Hypnosis

"*Creating With The Divine* is a wonderful book for someone beginning their healing or spiritual journey who feels stuck or paralyzed at a crossroads. This book is rich with faith and wisdom to live as your beloved truest self in every moment."

-Theresa Gutierrez
The 11th Hour Shaman

"The content of this book does a fantastic job of working in sequence through so many of the impediments one confronts when simply trying to organize the mind. It gives incredibly helpful suggestions and strategies for accomplishing this most daunting task. The pitfalls are recognized, confronted, and neutralized. This information leaves the realm of contemplation and very realistically enters the realm of considered action. I feel changed by reading this most thoughtful and complete book."

-Gene O'Neill
Master Musician

"The stories are relatable to anyone who has been gaslit and told to tone things down. Jumping Mouse was gaslit, but held the faith and said, screw it, I'll get new friends. When he knew helping his new friends would make him go blind, he let his faith lead the way and regained his sight. We don't need to know everything or see everything ahead of time, we just have to have the faith that we can pick the path we want to be on. I loved the suggestions in the book on how to get unstuck since they are simple and practical, and anyone can apply them."

-Christine Baker
LMT, NKT, Clinical Pain Specialist

"Honestly, I needed this book. For me it became a testimonial to my own wanderings, which have been many. Anyone who has felt lost, who has thought they may have just been chasing a dream, will take comfort in the story and glory of Jumping Mouse. We are here to explore, to learn, and to grow. Thank you, Reno & Janine. I've waited a long time to find my own confirmation. Simply speaking, Jumping Mouse is it!!!"

-Sherrie Waltz
Home Health Practitioner

"Ladies, you are the Dynamic Duo. I immediately felt the power and presence of your souls in the first chapter. You invited me into your portal of the Realms Within. The tears, laughter, and tools to succeed are within your personal stories. I appreciate your truth. For this I have much gratitude. "

-Nicole Borghi
Voice Over Artist, Commercial Creatrix

"I highly recommend this book to others. Jumping Mouse had a lot of impact on me."

-Will Anderson
Information Tech Specialist & Shaman

"I loved this book. I can relate jumping mouse's experiences to my life. From the animals he meets to the people in my life. I love this story. It brought tears to my eyes as I read it."

-Candice H. Beta-reader

"Creating With the Divine has come at the perfect time for me. I have been feeling stuck for the last several weeks. From the moment this book was brought to my attention, I felt an exciting energy pulling me to drink it up and Spirit wasn't going to allow me to say no. I am grateful for the support from Janine and Reno, their stories, and the tools they have shared, allowing me to move forward more easily on my journey. I definitely recommend this book for anyone who has a longing to feel alive!"

-Tawnya Hagan
Fire Keeper & Medium

"This book is helping me move from a place of fear into a firm place of action. It's helped me let go of my fear and embrace the passion that I have for my life. It's helping me see my path more clearly."

-Chere Hampton
Collective Care Coordinator & Community
Specialist

ALSO BY JANINE BOLON

DEDICATION

Reno Dedicates this book to:
The Great Creator Source for the provision and
awareness of all the synchronicities of the journey
and friendships.

Janine Dedicates this book to:
Dana Cain.
The event coordinator who put two-wheel walkers
together at the Athena Festival. Thank you!

CONTENTS

Chapter #9

ACKNOWLEDGEMENTS

A big thank you goes out to Mike Capuzzi and his team at Bite Sized Books who helped Reno and I get this book into their hands so quickly. Without them it would have taken us much longer to get this manuscript to press.

Also, thank you to the 53 beta readers who signed up to assist us with the flow of the book and the organization of the chapters. All of them were instrumental in how well this book reads; whether they listened to the audio tracks only or commented on the written portions of the book, they kept the content moving along.

A special shout out to the international members of the Crow Lodges, Divine MasterMinds and Workshop Participants that we have held over the past ten years. We learned and listened to intimate experiences of others in their walk with the Divine as we honed our own spiritual gifts. It has been an amazing journey hearing all of your stories.

Reno would like to express her thanks to all of you who have enriched her life by your presence, exchange of energy and spiritual understanding. She thanks the mentors, educators, seekers, and out-of-the-box thinkers. To her family, close friends, and countless clients, she thanks them for their encouragement and support in all her pursuits and passions!

Lastly, Janine wishes to thank her children: Sean, Matthias, James, and Clare – because of your perspectives, I was able to embrace the work I needed to do while being a mom to all of you. Your understanding and laughter have kept me going despite the challenges life throws our way!!

Our Fabulous Contributing Beta Readers:

Chere Hampton, Will Anderson, Tawnya Hagan, Gene O'Neill, Susan Barnum, Becky Lee, Candice H., Christine Baker, Jaron Bentley, Sandy L., Diana Davis, Theresa G., Brigitte, Sherrie Waltz, Trea F., Laura Davis, Anna D., Deborah H., Mark Siegel, Theresa M., and Susan Dworkin.

Master Mystic

noun

A person who has achieved by meditation or self-introspection unity with or integration into their Source.

They know who they are and continue to become more expansive with each day they live. Master Mystics can manifest into their lives all that they need and desire.

CHAPTER 1

STANDING AT THE CENTER OF THE CROSS ROAD

This is not a book for the masses. This book is highly specific to you. Reno LongMoons and I knew there would be people coming into our lives that would relish having a bit of clarity as they moved into the active creation of their own life.

We wrote this book for you.

We knew you were coming into our world and we wanted to share a bit about ourselves before you got to the delightful work of building the next phase of your life. We know you will have fun doing this work and we know that there are times when you feel like you have a mess of things, but know this: Reno and I know the power, skill sets, and imagination that you bring into each moment of your life.

We have been guiding women's circles, retreats, and ceremonies for decades. Roughly 60+ years of facilitating men and women through the crossroads of transformation. We know that every human on the planet has a point in their lives where a tough, life-altering decision must be made. As they stand at the hub of that decision, they see four pathways stretched before them.

They can move straight ahead. Along a predetermined path that looks safe and secure, but also leaves their heart feeling heavier and not as fulfilled. There is also the path behind them; they know that road all too well and it would only repeat their previous life experiences. They have no wish to do that.

Then there are the paths to their left and to their right. No matter which direction they look, they see nothing that distinguishes one path from the other. The visual cues are not there to guide them. All is a flatland filled with the same barren landscape, but they need to make a decision. They feel the call in their heart and in their soul. It is a restlessness that they need more, they need to seek more. What is this more? They don't know. The best that they know to say is that they are stuck, they are restless, they want "out" of the loop that they feel they are in.

You, dear reader, may find yourself having been through such a process. And in moving out of that hub of indecision you reached out and the Universe found a way to get this book into your hands. Reno and I applaud you. We know how far you have come. We know how difficult some of your decisions have been. We now offer you additional support and guidance as you move into the next realm of your life. We will happily facilitate this transformation.

We wrote this book because of a sacred ceremony that was held in 2019. We had a group of 21 women sitting in a living room in Colorado. It was the time of the Fall Equinox. A time to release, let go and shed all those things; physical, mental, emotional, and spiritual that no longer serves your life. As the ceremony was wrapping up, someone asked me about my writing: "How is the book trilogy coming along, Janine?" I answered that all three were complete and I was doing final edits on the third book to send out to the publisher. It was then that Reno LongMoons responded, "There will be a fourth." Now, this was the last thing I wanted to hear. I had no intention of writing a fourth book for the "Divine Series." However, I knew that if something is said in Sacred Ceremony, I need to listen to that prompting. It took three more years of ceremonies, meetings, and synchronicities to finally bring about this book that is now in your hands.

We knew what we needed to share with you, but the process and timing was elusive to us. We knew you would have entered our lives for a very specific reason, and it took us much praying and discovery to realize what it was we could offer you that would bring you comfort, direction, and a sense of relief from the challenges of life.

In November of 2022, it became clear we needed to share with you an ancient story of transformation and inner trust. We needed to share the story of Jumping Mouse and the metaphors that the story brings into our way of processing the inner journey of self-trust along with the physical, mental, emotional, and spiritual transformations that occur as you move through your decision-making in creating the life that you know you need to live.

THIS IS OUR BOOK

This book has multiple components to it. It is a multimedia book due to the nature of the storytelling and information within it. There are multiple chapters in this book that will walk you through tools and techniques on how to move through your life with ease and a bit more relaxation than you may have ever thought possible. Some of the storytelling is not done with the written word, but it is done via audio files because it is tradition that some of the story needs to be shared verbally. Here you will find QR codes and website links that will lead you to audio files for those particular sections.

Also, the story of Jumping Mouse and his transformation is an integral part of education for the young and old alike in many tribes. These sorts of stories were told during the wintertime when the nights were longer than the days. People would gather as the sun set to enjoy their community around the warmth of a fire. The storytellers would then begin their work of education and entertainment to the people through their origin stories.

This book is a guide that you can use to walk out of the crossroads of indecision and confusion and into inspired action for your life's journey.

CHAPTER 2

JUMPING MOUSE—A STORY OF TRANSFORMATION

The Stories We Learn

Throughout our childhood we are gifted stories of principles and behavior that shape how we view life as well as interact with it. Some stories are designed to protect you from harm; such as the activity of wandering alone in the forest like Hansel and Gretel, or stories of caution like the Spider and the Fly.

Elders have been protecting the young and teaching their history through the art of storytelling for millennia. The story of *Jumping Mouse* is one that is common among the Iroquois League which is a recognized confederacy and is made up of the six nations: Mohawk, Oneida, Ogananda, Seneca, Cayuga, and Tuscarora. Reno LongMoons is a citizen of the Seneca Nation and shares with us the version of *Jumping Mouse* as it comes to her memory and her storytelling art.

Like all good classic stories, *Jumping Mouse* carries within it the truth of transmutation and trust. Different nations, different storytellers, and different situations will highlight various aspects of the story based upon the needs of the particular audience. I have witnessed Reno's storytelling abilities on several occasions and marveled at her craft of story based upon the young people present or the more elderly women of her tribe. This is the art and craft of the elder storyteller: being able to take the bones of a story and mend the structure to the best benefit of the listeners in need of a certain metaphor in their own lives.

It is an honor and privilege to be a part of this process of bringing *Jumping Mouse* to you today in this mixed media format. Here is the QR code to listen to Reno's retelling of *Jumping Mouse*:

Or you may type this link into your web browser and listen that way.

https://thepracticalmystics.com/
jumping-mouse/

After Reno worked with me for 15 days sharing her stories and perspectives on *Jumping Mouse*, I asked her more personal questions about her own experiences with the story as she integrates it into her life's journey.

My first question to her was: **When did you first hear Jumping Mouse, Reno?**

When I first heard it, I was a kid. I don't remember exactly when I heard it. I enjoyed hearing about *Jumping Mouse*. It was just an exciting adventure story. It had no impact whatsoever that I knew of at the time. Other than that, it was an adventure story about this little mouse – what he went through, who he met – and it was all happy making. I think I had the same reactions to the story as I see in my grandchildren when I tell it to them. They're like, "Aww, what a good story, I enjoyed that." Just a kid's perspective of enjoying the story and moving on.

But it sticks with you. It really sticks with you. There are elements of recurring truth in it.

When did the story change for you? As you got older, it started making an impact on you. Would you walk us through the impact of the Jumping Mouse story?

Jumping Mouse came alive for me around ages 15-17. Many of my spiritual gifts had been negated many times by friends and family. I kept hearing things, yet people around me couldn't hear what I was hearing. That was when _Jumping Mouse_ came back in for me and when I spoke about it, people around me were like, "No, I don't think that's real" and "I think that you're making that up." Those experiences are my first recollection I have of feeling different. I felt I needed to figure out what was wrong with me. Why are people telling me things about me that aren't true? And that's when the story of _Jumping Mouse_ came back into memory.

The part about his community not believing and not caring what he was hearing, and it was just like mine. That is where it was all similar. People didn't care. They were suggesting to me, "Just be a normal mouse. Just be normal. Just be a normal person. Don't be different. Don't be unique."

I remember feeling really frustrated by the world around me. I felt negated in many ways, and I was trying to find my own truth. That is like a dark alley and you walk alone in that for a while. Because you know you're not crazy, and you're adamant in having to prove to yourself that you are what you are.

Jumping Mouse kept coming back into my life through memory as well as through companions. Not in the form of a person, but in the form of a book. I was trying really hard to figure out what's going on here, and why am I different? Why am I annoyed by certain things in the world?

During this time of my life there was a huge wave of "excuse abuse" in my environment. Everybody had an excuse for something, and the excuse abuse was crazy. It was almost like, if I have the proper excuse, I have a free pass to be stupid. It wasn't just victim excuses; it was general excuses, and that frustrated me. I didn't understand why there was no accountability, I guess you might say, because here I am on this road; I've got to figure out where I am so I can talk about where I am because people don't believe where I am. I need to have some points of reference to be able to share.

I then came across a book written by Dr. Wayne Dyer, called, "Living Responsibly in an Age of Excuses." (editorial note: The Updated Version of this book is called Excuses Begone!) That book answered a lot of questions for me and on the heels of reading that book, *Jumping Mouse* came back in. And all the frustrations that I had felt about people using excuse abuse and not being held accountable for their own set of stuff fell away as I looked within myself and said, "Okay, what am I excusing, what am I here to do?"

And *Jumping Mouse* said, "Well, you know you're on this journey to figure out who you are and what you are, and it's all about you. You've got to be able to listen to where you are being led."

That was the spiritual calling for me. Spirit was saying, "Hey, guess what? Time to take a trek down your lane. Go find out what is calling at you and what makes you the unique individual you are. And that is when my true spiritual questing started. I realized I wasn't alone. I heard things that I didn't understand and I needed to find out more about. That desire was rejected so strongly while I was younger that it fueled my questing to seek out answers. In lots of different ways, looking for answers and trusting people around me who I didn't know very well helped me get where I wanted to be. Ultimately it was my choice to make the trek, but some things are so deep that it doesn't allow you to NOT choose it. You still have to just get to a moment of, "Okay, I've gotta go with this."

Please share a bit about finding the written story of Jumping Mouse.

Oh, I found the written story of *Jumping Mouse* at a thrift store. I picked up the book to see if it aligned to what my memory was. And man, the way that Mary Elizabeth Marlow writes this book; it shares the story and the stories of others. It was super impactful because I felt like everything that I had learned and remembered in the journey that was the last several years of my time, it all just solidified. It all just made sense. It was that "Aha!" moment. It explains the actions and the heart's desire to know more and to find out who you really are, and the rewards for doing exactly that.

The seeking of truth and understanding was focused into my moment. This moment of finding the written word gave me permission to seek. My parents were great at allowing us kids to seek understanding before choosing a specific path. They wanted us to believe in something so we were exposed to a variety of religions. There are so many things that I think you fall in and out of questing as your life morphs and as things change and you try to figure out who you are, what you want to represent. Ultimately, it comes down to you being honest with you. What do you see?

At this phase of your life right now, how do you see *Jumping Mouse*?

I feel like my path over the years has mirrored *Jumping Mouse*'s story. I've been able to be at peace with the gifts that I've been given and to find the community with whom I can share those gifts and that allows me to be me, because my community now allows me to be me. But most importantly, I got to the place of giving myself permission to be me. To accept myself just the way that I am and with the struggles with the everydayness of me and through the spiritual side of me.

When do you feel you became Eagle in your life?

I became Eagle when I went through the Ascended Masters course, I became Eagle when I started teaching others, I became Eagle when I could remove myself from my own situation and look at different options. I became Eagle at lots of different times in my life. When I became a parent, I had to teach my little hatchling, ya know? I'm still becoming an Eagle.

Jumping Mouse is a story that is appropriate at any point in your life. Because there are times you're going to be in that group of non-acceptance or non-caring about the excitement that you have over something, and I find that it's okay that someone else doesn't understand where I am. I understand where I am.

I had lots of great mentors that came into my life that not only validated what I was feeling but helped me understand why I had these inspirations, feelings, and knowings. What I was sensing and the spiritual gifts that I had were understood through the perspectives of these great mentors of mine. I learned not only what I was supposed to do with my gifts, but why I had them. Some of my mentors stayed in my life for a long, long time, even to today, and others didn't. I have comfort with the knowledge and that is an Eagle moment.

Jumping Mouse is a recurring element and application in my life. *Jumping Mouse* is what I use as a guide. Am I in a community that understands me? No? Well then go find the right community. Do I need help with this? Yes? Go find Raccoon that can lead me to where I need to get my answers and resources.

I've had those people in my life and I've had the people that were strong enough to tell me what to do, I did it, I believed them and came up out of the water sputtering and belligerent, "You betrayed me!" And really that wasn't the reality.

There are a variety of times when the story comes back into my life. It comes back with ways for me to recognize where I am on my path. I use it as a tool to help me understand where I am and that the ultimate goal in any moment is to become the Eagle of Clarity.

How to Use the Story of Jumping Mouse in Your Own Life

Jumping Mouse is a story we can all relate to at various times in our lives. Below is the path or journey that each soul can take while here on planet Earth. The journey of self-evolution is also one of self-creation. You are creating with the Divine with each choice you make in your life and with each person who becomes a part of your path. Here is a quick outline of the *Jumping Mouse* story as it moves us through the journey of self-discovery and trust.

You can use this outline as a marker of where you are or where you wish to go next. You may feel like you are stuck at the hub of the wheel, but in actuality, you are moving along your path. Who do you need to find for the next part of your journey or is this a time for you to figure out your next steps? This outline will be a guide for you to determine what you need next.

A Step-by-Step Outline of *Jumping Mouse*

Origin - A Mouse Doing Mouse Things

Mouse: Being a mouse and doing mouse things, then...

Loud Noise: Great Spirit gives a call to mouse.

Mouse: Community does not hear what mouse hears.

Awakening - Leaves Community as Mouse - What is the noise?

Raccoon: Gives advice & guidance to a river and is the first teacher.

Frog: Jump and tell me what you see. It is going to be amazing, cheerleader and encourager.

Mouse: Sees Sacred Mountain and lands in the river. Comes out feeling betrayed.

Mad at Frog: Betrayer, bemused at mouse's distress

Frog: What did you see?

Source of Noise was seen: The Sacred Mountain.

Mouse now is renamed: *Jumping Mouse*, he has been changed by his vision.

Returns to Community as *Jumping Mouse*

Community: Just be Mouse-no celebration of Jumping Mouse's Return.

Jumping Mouse: Attempts to go back to normal - attempts to live in community-no one listens.

Jumping Mouse: Can't stay-a compulsion to journey to the Sacred Mountain (the call has been made & tugs at Jumping Mouse).

Second Adventure - Goal - Sacred Mountain - Where is the Noise?

Jumping Mouse: Courageous run into the prairie, meets a veteran mouse, older, wiser, gray haired.

Prairie Mouse: Offers rest, renewal, distraction.

Jumping Mouse: Needs to journey, needs to answer the call.

Prairie Mouse: Offers fear, discouragement, distraction.

Jumping Mouse: Faces fear and continues the journey.

Buffalo: Ill, sick and needs the eye of a mouse to be whole.

Jumping Mouse: Climbs on top of the horn of buffalo.

Jumping Mouse: Seeks advice from Prairie Mouse.

Jumping Mouse: Allows the eye to be taken for the Buffalo to become whole.

Buffalo: Offers to give Jumping Mouse a ride on his belly as protection from fears.

Buffalo: Delivers Jumping Mouse across the prairie and then recedes to his home.

Jumping Mouse: Scrambles up the mountain to the timber line and meets Wolf.

Wolf: Full of woe, memory issues, continuously returns to himself & his need for wholeness via the medicine of a mouse's eye.

Jumping Mouse: Gives Wolf his eye and is offered assistance through the wood.

Jumping Mouse: Blind and seeking is near the summit.

Frog: The summit has been achieved and the lake is before Jumping Mouse.

Frog: Offers refreshment, water, peace, stillness.

Jumping Mouse: Whoosh! Sound.

Transformation to Eagle-
I Am What I Fear Most

Eagle: No more *Jumping Mouse*.

Sacred Mountain: Heart of Great Spirit: Center of Your Creation.

CHAPTER 3

RELEASING YOUR BEAT-UP ROUTINES

The Stories We Accept

Reno and I want to remind you of a simple thing. You no longer need to beat yourself up for what you have done, what you haven't done, or what you should have done in your past.

You may have heard this over and over, but we want you to really integrate it now. You are not your past. What you did in the past was due to the information and training you had back then. You are now a different person, and it is time for you to value the person you are today rather than use your past to keep you beaten down and in a place of indecision. There are several sentences that I have used throughout my life that have moved me from a place of total analysis paralysis into inspired action. I will share some of those with you directly, but first, we need to clear the path for your highest and best good.

When you find yourself in a place where you just don't know what to do, it is time to release your trust issues and allow your heart to have a say in the matter, rather than allowing the mind to continue hijacking your decision-making process. Those 12 inches between your head and heart can really be a long road if you don't recognize the fact that your indecision is due to you being totally in your head. Allow yourself to remember that your head will lead you into a binary world of right-wrong, good-bad, love-hate, black-white sort of processing. It is designed to make decisions, but it is a search engine. If you ask yourself questions filled with guilt, shame and fear, your mind will search out those very things to add data to your matrix as you continue to work through the situation.

Example: Why is this awful situation happening to me?

Brain: Because [search engine queries every awful experience that you ever had] Let me go find every reason I can about why this is happening to you! You did something wrong, and we'll go look into every detail of what happened to prevent you from ever making this mistake again.

Wowzers! That's a powerful search engine, but it wasn't working in your favor, was it? So how do we get this powerful search engine to work FOR you?

Ask Yourself Different Questions

Ask yourself outcome-based questions: what does this mean? Instead of looking for reasons why you are in this mess, instead focus on the outcome you want and frame the question that way.

Example: Why is this current situation the best thing that is happening to me right now?

I used this one day in my past. I was remembering a painful time in my life when I was holding a crying baby and my father slapped me because I had spoken my truth about a friend of his who was mean. I was ten years old and there was a lot I could have unpacked about that event. Instead of focusing on the hurt, betrayal, and shock of the moment. I put my search engine to work on seeking out this answer:

"Janine, why was that past situation a good thing for me?" Immediately, my brain went to work on why this was a good thing. It came up with the following:

- It taught me I have no control over how someone will react to what I say
- It taught me my words have power that I didn't fully understand

I have used this technique with many of my clients and each one is stunned by what their own personal search engine has come up with regarding horrific situations in their past. Each one has found a measure of peace and calm over previously debilitating trauma. One extreme example was a young woman who had been recommended to me by her therapist. She was 24 years old and had been sexually abused by a family member. She had found a man she wanted to marry and was actively working to release her old traumas so she could begin a new life with her beloved.

After doing some foundational work and coordinating sessions with her therapist, I asked her to meditate and go into her safe place. I then asked her, "Why was that situation a good thing for you?" Her therapist just stared at me! She quickly responded, "Well, I don't know, it was all so messed up and... it gave me more compassion for people. They don't always have control of the environments they are in." Her eyes snapped open and she looked at me startled, and a quiet, "Wow." came from her lips.

This is a super extreme example, and we are not talking about quick fixes. She was still under the care of a medical team after I left her journey, but there are points where a pivotal question stated in terms of the "outcome" you wish to have is more powerful than dissecting the whys and wherefores of a situation that you had no control in. Right?

Take the time to listen to yourself and how your thoughts are leading you. When you find yourself asking questions, be mindful of where your powerful search engine is taking you. Is it really an outcomes-based question you are asking, or are you just sending yourself down a rabbit hole of darkness, shame, guilt and loathing?

Another question I like to ask my clients when I hear them in beat-up routines is this:

"Would you ever say this to a friend?

Then why are you saying this to yourself? Again, what is the outcome you wish for yourself on this life journey?"

Last question before we move onto some tools. When you find yourself belittling your life or talking bad about yourself on the way you handled a past situation, please remember this question:

Would You Say This to a Child?

Remember we grew up with our personal understanding of who we are being questioned, denied, or challenged by people bigger, louder and stronger than ourselves. We know from our own experiences that when speaking to children, you are molding not only their thoughts of themselves but of their worldview.

Speak well of yourself. Speak gently to yourself. Speak kindly of your path. When you do this, it smooths out those potholes and barriers and makes them into small dips and speed bumps.

Now, let's get you some tools to work with when you find yourself needing a bit more than questions to move out of your head and into your heart.

Reno has a whole bag of tools she uses to move out of confusion and into clarity. She calls them her "dark tools" because she is focused on bringing her thoughts out of the darkness of confusion and into the light of clarity.

Reno's Dark Tools

Let's take a look at ways that confusion, along with the other items listed, can and often be presented. It may come in a different form for each individual, so take time to look at what this may mean for you.

When you know or sense something that you need to do or work on, but you are unclear what the next step should be.

Mixed messages externally and internally:

Externally–What you are seeing doesn't align with what you believe to be true. Yet you do see that the methodology of the result appears to be working for others in a similar circumstance – this is perspective – take a pause, step back, and view with an open mind.

Internally–You know what needs to be done but hesitate on the method to accomplish the task at hand. Self-doubt and negative self dialogue trigger the lack of execution.

TOOLS of CLARITY:

Dark Tools

Dark tools are the tools that lay dormant until they are required. Many times, we are unaware that these tools are available and ready for utilization. They present themselves upon being triggered. In some instances these can be tools carried over from past experiences that we have resolved, and in that resolution, we learned a better way to move forward and in doing so, acquired a skill or tool that aids us.

- **Knee-jerk reactions**: This is a great place to stop and look at what triggered a reaction that was seemingly out of character for the way you perceive yourself. The tool is aware-ness in a way that you have not utilized prior.
- **Fear**: This is the type of fear that brings on motivation – creating action and momen-tum. Typically fear has the following flight, fight, or flee responses, but in the case of dark tools, it is more of an enCOURAGEr to step out and to take control of YOURSELF

and choose your next step. Unlike the flight, fight, or flee responses that we have been told about, this is a calculated movement on your part and empowers you with a positive outcome. Not to negate the three "F"s; those are more instinctual responses rather than mindful responses.

- **Script flipping**: This is an exceptionally strong dark tool. Catching yourself when your internal dialogue is picking apart everything and has lead you so far away from what is actually the issue at hand. The flip occurs when you employ the techniques of celebrating and appreciating how you over-came other difficult aspects that you had experienced. Self-appreciation is key here to embracing the amazing individual that you have become. Affirmations, meditations, remembrances, and celebrations of accomplishments are great ways to achieve this.

- **"The Land of *What If*"**: A great place to visit but not to take up residency. Take a brief walk down the path to this place of, "If I do this, these are the possible outcomes for those actions." While visiting Land of What If, avoid making the comparison to what others did in their journey on the path. Your results will not always mirror that of others.

Example of Knee-Jerk Reactions

In my own life I have caught myself in a reaction that completely took me by surprise. Trust me, this has been on more than one occasion, and continues to be a place now that I welcome because I know growth for my betterment is at hand.

I have to stop and ask myself, where did that come from? For instance, I was working on a project that meant a lot to me, and the individual who was to approve and move forward with this particular project came back and said that it was nowhere near what was requested. Immediately, I became defensive and angry. That was my knee-jerk reaction. There are qualities in this example that did not align with my version of who I thought I was. Instead, I reacted out of being negated and rejected. Of course, in the moment, clarity was not at my fingertips. It took looking at the knee-jerk reaction to understand where and why it presented. I needed to understand what had happened was something I was not pleased with, and how to bring that into alignment with my current self-vision. In doing so, I had to recognize that I still had rawness in being negated. I also had to take accountability of my current reaction and find a new, positive way to handle those situations. I know now that taking a moment to pause before reacting – and presenting things in the way I WANT to be seen (in alignment with my present self) – is paramount. Gleaning for the good and looking at what is in your control to correct or adapt to bring into harmony the SELF that you see and want to be, is what helps when the knee-jerk reaction comes to play.

Example of Script Flipping

Script flipping comes into play when I realize that I am my own personal opponent in my thoughts. I have caught myself tearing apart my self-worth with questions like, "Who do you think you are really? What makes you so qualified to do the work you are doing?" These are all said with an extreme condescending tone. The way that I CHOOSE (that action is KEY to flipping the dialogue) to combat those moments is to begin listing the accomplished/completed things that have happened. For example, my first women's retreat – facilitating, hosting, marketing, and providing for an OUTDOOR camping environment. I had many moments when those questions played over and over and over again. In this example, the need outweighed the insecurities that I had been feeling. I focused on the need and benefit for others outside myself. Now there are additional retreats that have been done and the war in my thoughts is replaced with greater confidence.

Example of The Land of *What If*:

Often I will be thinking of a scenario that I am involved in that may include other individuals. In this I am attempting to role play both sides of either the conversation or the situation. Words of extreme caution when in the land of what if: remember these thoughts are NOT reality; that you are providing conversation or reaction for someone else; this is neither fair or realistic as these words and reactions may never be said in the real world as related to the situation. Be diligent to ensure that you will be able to listen completely to the ACTUAL dialogue in real time. Another caution is directed to you. You must guard against allowing yourself to believe that what happens in the land of what if does not become the belief you are carrying. Having been in this precarious position, I have found that this is a great place to run through POSSIBLE outcomes such as, "If I do this, then MAYBE this will happen," or, "This could be a bad outcome," either way. This is a land that can be cultivated for creative out-of-the-box thinking to expand optional variables safely.

CHAPTER 4

DON'T JUST DO SOMETHING, SIT THERE!

Motivation vs Inspiration–When to Act!

There are times in our seeking of clarity and an action plan that we can seek out experiences for motivation. Our desire to have clarity in our lives can lead us to act way before it is good for us to do so. One of the things I coach my clients on is the need for inspiration, not motivation.

Action is not always your friend, especially when you are in a mental state of fear. When you're being threatened, of course you will use motivation to move out of harm's way, but inspired action is what is needed from you for the crossroads of life. How do you make sure to use inspired action rather than motivation for your decision-making processes?

Inspired action causes one of two emotions when you are thinking of your potential pathways. Inspired action stirs within you excitement or enthusiasm. There is no resistance to the idea. You light up when you think of the possibility of your new direction. It isn't until you start to think of, "how am I going to make this happen?" that the mind gets involved and causes you to move down the emotional ladder into despondency. You have no idea how to move forward on your inspiration or you put up too much resistance to the path that has been shown to you. Your search engine is seeking out all the reasons you shouldn't move forward. This is not good for you.

Reno's Suggestion:

Sometimes, all the right ingredients are not yet in place to build the success that you are envisioning. This is why NOT doing something can play an important role as you move forward. This all sounds very counter-intuitive, but time in these instances is truly your ally.

Allowing yourself to first recognize and understand that at that particular moment you are not required to do anything provides the perspective to see when action is needed and what action will be required.

Jump First, Learn to Swim Later

It is not always necessary to know what you are doing when it comes to your own life. There are times when all you need to do is take a few moments to figure out what you DO want in your life and just act. If you have a situation you have been wanting to do, then act on that inspiration. Most especially if you find yourself in an uplifted emotional state. There are many times that you won't know if you really find that experience fun until you get yourself into the middle of it.

Janine's Example:

I found after 40 years of saying "no" to myself, it was time to learn how to play the piano. I went online and found an old keyboard that was being sold at a very reasonable rate and purchased it. Then I downloaded an app onto my tablet and set it up on my keyboard and began to play according to the directions. Now that all sounds so very simple and easy, doesn't it? Well, this is what it looked like in real time.

Step 1: Go online and look up the best keyboards for beginners learning to play. I had my own requirements for this keyboard. It had to:

- Have all 88 keys.
- Have a headphone jack.

- Be able to play out loud.
- Be able to plug into a computer and record.
- Be easy to move from room-to-room.
- Be under $250.

Step 2: Go online and look for a used keyboard close to what I researched.

Step 3: Found the keyboard and negotiated terms with the seller.

Step 4: Download an app onto my tablet so I could start teaching myself how to play. Requirements for the app:

- I needed lessons that tracked my progress.
- I wanted to learn songs that had been pre-recorded so I knew what they sounded like as I was playing them.
- After researching different software packages and apps, I settled on a program that did all the things I needed.
- Bought the app (free apps wouldn't track my progress nor had the options I wanted).

Step 5: Keyboard arrived in the home. I had already cleared a space for it so it was easily brought into the house and immediately set up so I could start learning.

Step 6: Started learning to play and had a sense of accomplishment since I could finally find center "C." That was lesson one.

Small, little steps are all that is needed to make your life move in the direction that you want. We have the ability now to achieve most anything we wish to accomplish. The decision is this; do you have the courage to move in the direction of your dreams? For many, it isn't courage they need. It is clarity. They know they want more out of life. They know they wish to move in a different direction, but they have no idea what that is. Stay tuned and we'll help you get there.

Anything Is Better Than Nothing

Then there are those times in life where it is better that you act! It is better that you do SOMETHING rather than just sit and do nothing. This tells you that you are waiting for the pain of your situation to reach a certain point before you will act. If you continue to sit and do nothing, you'll fall into anger where you are barking harshly at everyone, or worse: you'll sink into depression or despondency. We don't want you to do either. It is at those times that there are a few quick questions you can ask yourself to help you over the speed bump that is slowing your momentum down or has you feeling stuck.

When you find yourself sparking off with anger or you are triggered into anger, realize there are two things that are assumptions from your unconscious mind. Understand that anger is usually due to:

1. I'm afraid I'm not going to get what I want
2. My expectations have not been met by this situation

During one of our Crow Lodges in 2018, Reno suggested that when we find ourselves in anger, we take a few deep breaths, calm ourselves the best we can, and dig into those unmet expectations and fears.

Reno's Questions for Working Through Fear, Anxiety, or Distress:

Am I open to my Truth?
Am I ready to release this Fear?
What do I need to release this Fear?
Do I have the tools to release this Fear?

Fear likes you to think you are alone.
This is false.

When you are dealing with the can't see the forest through the trees effect, reach out to a trusted friend or professional. It's been my experience that having an outside perspective introduces and interrupts the mental looping of the same thoughts.

Break it down, take it a step at a time. You will know when you have resolved the issue that makes you feel like you are being held back when it no longer has the power to hold you.

Take time to appreciate and celebrate each step of accomplishment. Allow this method to be applied to smaller accomplishments. The act of acknowledging the completion fuels the momentum. This also holds true for the larger accomplishments. We have a tendency to focus on the bigger accomplishments and forget the small ones that lead us to success.

https://thepracticalmystics.com/expressing-the-divine-printables/

CHAPTER #5

WHAT DO I WANT?

This is the chapter you've been waiting for. This is where you bring yourself into laser focus with your dreams, desires, and destinations for yourself. Many of these processes were covered in my book *Expressing the Divine: A Guidebook for the Enlightened Soul*. But we will quickly recap them here for you as well.

There is a downloadable document that is a journaling tool. You are welcome to use it as you read along. You can find it by using the QR code or link on page 44.

The most important question for this section is #10 from page 1 of the downloadable document.

What Would I Do If I Knew I Couldn't Fail?

That is my best question for moving myself out of fear and into a heart-centered space to start dreaming of my future life; not as a place to escape to when situations were harsh and difficult, but as a target for me to plan and take action toward. Many of us know what we don't want, but this also guides us perfectly on what we do want. Right? If you knew you couldn't fail, what is it that you would allow yourself to dream about, attempt, or learn?

Many times, the answer is quite obvious. "Janine, what is it that you really want?" If you struggle to answer that question, then I recommend you go down to your local library. Find the non-fiction stacks in the adult section. Slowly walk through the stacks and as various books catch your eye, pull them off the shelves and start to read. Glance at pictures and just scan some of the table of contents. Take two hours to run through the stacks and just allow yourself to wander, scan, browse, and learn. This is like you wandering through the forest of your unconscious mind, and you have access to that infinite knowledge. Before you know it, you will be headed into certain areas of the library and will find a whole new range of knowledge that intrigues you and you didn't even know there were THAT many people writing on that particular topic!

I've run through this exercise with four of my clients. One of them was so resistant to books due to a troubled childhood where reading was seen as a punishment, not a blessing. We managed to get into the library despite her protests. Within minutes she was stunned by the sheer volume of books on the shelves. She no longer saw them as inanimate, lifeless volumes of print, but she felt the forest of knowledge as the energy of all those books began to speak to her and call her toward her Higher Wisdom. She is the one who shared with me that walking through a library is now her version of walking through a forest. If she can't get out into nature, she goes to her local library to be surrounded by all the trees that have been immortalized in print and books. What a beautiful way to transform your mindset, don't you think?

Reno Suggests:

If you are having difficulty answering the question, "What do I want?" here are suggestions that may be helpful.

Look for recurring themes in your life that hold passion and desire. These are often ideas or actions that create a desire to go from spectator to participant. Whether it is volunteering or creating a community of like-minded meetups or gathering, or even pursuing a business utilizing your spiritual gifts: these are suggestions that are to encourage you to be in a relationship with your higher self. You have the power of options and choice.

CHAPTER 6

YOU ARE YOUR OWN
BEST DECISION MAKER

Visionaries Are Their Own #1 Fan

People who are visionaries have changed the world. When we think of visionaries, often the people that come to mind are:

- John D. Rockefeller, Sr.
- Marie Curie
- Walt Disney
- Mother Teresa
- Gandhi
- Martin Luther King, Jr.
- Steve Jobs
- Sara Lomelin
- Elon Musk

They are people who see problems and then start solving them even if society, at large, is not ready for their solutions. They are their own best fans. They are so passionate about what they see as the life they want, they never back down from their dream. It is too ingrained in their realities they see for themselves and the people around them. Whether you agree with their philosophy, solution, or oratory is not the point. These people are admired for their willingness to move toward their dreams with a passion and direction that is laser focused.

Now, don't confuse laser focus with "knowing." Visionaries rarely know what they are doing every step of the way. They walk through the land of uncertainty just like the rest of us. The difference is, they are their own #1 fan. Their charisma is contagious because they so firmly believe in what they are doing and where they are going in their lives. "How" they are going to do it – well, that is always evolving before them. But their direction and the target are fixed.

How can you become your own best fan? It begins with a mirror.

Looking in the Mirror, Can You Say, "I Love You?"

This is an exercise in authenticity and trust. Can you look at yourself in a mirror and lean in real close so that you are looking into your own eyes, and then say in a whisper to yourself,

"I love you."

For some mystics, this took seven to nine days before they could do it without crying. For others, they were able to do it in a day or two. The point is this: love yourself and you can change the world. No kidding. When you have the ability to love yourself, "warts and all" as my granny used to say, then you are on the road to power, change, and transformation. This form of knowing is your place of power. You know your own heart. You know all that you have wished for and what you are accomplishing each day despite huge speed bumps in your life. No one else knows what you know about yourself.

Here is where your power center is. Being able to look at yourself and love yourself through and through. You are a human being on planet Earth, and loving all the aspects that make you all that you are allows you to bring more manifestation into this three-dimensional reality. Once you love yourself, then you start to trust yourself to make the right decisions in all that you do.

Building Personal Trust

Some of my clients have told me that they have a hard time believing that they can trust themselves when they have a difficult time picking their partners or choosing the best path to follow. That is when we start discussing their emotional guidance system they have. Over and over in our lives we have wanted to follow a specific path and were detoured by other people's opinions, fears, and cautions.

Realize that you are now in a position where you will make good decisions for yourself if you will harmonize your thinking with your heart's desires. We'll discuss the processes you can use for that in the next chapter.

CHAPTER 7

HARMONIZING THE HEART AND THE MIND

The Stories We Share

How you speak about yourself and what you discuss with others will determine the next set of people, places, and experiences you attract into your life.

Please reread that part again. What comes into your life next is based upon how you view yourself and the stories you've been sharing with others. One of the most powerful points of creation you have in this world is how you feel about your life. Your ability to define for yourself what you want out of life will directly affect the path your life will take. We like to call this portion of life direction "Building Your Own Story." No matter what has happened to you in the past, no matter what stories you have currently been sharing, the most powerful technique we can share with you today (after meditation) is this:

You attract what you think/feel about and what you talk about.

The more you speak about the beautiful blue glass that you saw in a shop window, the more and more you will see blue glass manifesting in your world. Now your analytical mind may say to you, "Yes, but those items have always been there, you just see them now." Does it matter? Not really. No matter what the fact may be, you now see what you are creating around you. You are now aware of how you are speaking to others, the stories that you are telling to others, and you are now taking yourself into account.

You are the primary factor in your life creation.

It is important to define for yourself the life you would like to live so that you can then decide on what you wish to attract into your world.

Building Your Own Story– Create Your Bus Route

No matter where you have been, no matter the previous choices you have made: you can make a difference now in your life situation. It won't take a lot of effort on your part. It won't take a lot of energy. It will actually take you letting go of some previously held ideas you created for yourself that are no longer serving you.

This is not about digging deep in your past. This is not about finding out the dark shadows that are hiding in your subconscious mind. This is about you making a primary change in your life. Is it time for you to take charge of your life? Is it time for you to start driving your own bus?

Are You Driving Your Bus?

For most of our lives we are told the path that we need to take by well-meaning (and not-so-well-meaning) people. When we are children we may accept this guidance so that we avoid pain and suffering, but as we age we learn that people often will tell us things out of their own fears, uncertainties, or fatigue. They aren't really thinking about us at all when they offer their guidance. Or they are making some huge assumptions about what our life is like and what we lived through to achieve our current situation.

At some point in your life you learned that people, in general, didn't have a clue on the best way for you to live your life, and it was now time for you to make your own decisions. I like to call this phase "getting off others' bus." You may have spent too long on this particular route of your life, or you have found that you are on a different route, or you are wanting to see a different section of the city.

Because my father was in the Navy and I was able to travel the world with him, I saw so many different ways that people viewed life, lived in various societies, and operated as individuals in heterogeneous populations. It became apparent to my young mind that there were many different ways of living, but as I moved about the United States, I started to see different regions of the country had different ways of viewing what it meant to be American, and how you were to act in those particular regions.

The same is true for us as we travel about our communities as we move through life. We are more than willing to travel along with a group of people on the same bus since we may not know where we are going. We may even find the ride enjoyable with the people we are on the bus with, but at some point, you realize that this particular bus driver is not going where you wish to go, and it is time for you to drive your own bus.

Determining Your Own Route

When you make the decision to live life according to your own rules and to take a route that you've never taken before, it can be downright terrifying; but I want you to know this is also the quickest path to getting what you want out of life. When you are determined to get to a destination of your own design, you will take a path that many others fear to tread. It is one of those times when you are doing something out of the ordinary for yourself. This is new and different and in perfect alignment with the type of person you wish to be rather than the type of person you thought yourself to be.

For years, all I could think about was the harmony and tranquility that I could manifest externally to myself. I was the eldest child in my family, and it was frequently my lot in life to handle situations in the family because of a terminally ill mother and an absentee father. I was one of the latch key children of the 80s where both parents worked, and I was often making decisions with no experience with to guide me. I had come up with a set of rules for my conduct and decision-making that served me well through high school and college based on my circumstances at home, but when I hit my 30s, that form of decision-making had to change drastically. I found myself working from home and tending to the needs of small children.

My entire life had evolved and changed, but I hadn't made the mental change in how I processed information and how I handled the chaotic aspects of four small children and me being the only adult around. I was comparing how I needed to raise my children in the 2000s with how my parents raised me, and there were drastic changes that needed to happen.

What are some of the patterns you see in your own thinking that no longer serve you?

This is the place where you need to go on your own bus now. To the place where you are aware of what you are thinking. Is this current line of thinking in alignment with the journey you want to take?

Reno Suggests:

Owning the bus–you are the bus. Owning the bus reminds you of the self-care (oil changes, tire rotations, and maintenance required) responsibility that you have to yourself. If your bus is the standard orange and black bus colors, and you would rather it be cherry red or all the colors of the rainbow, you CAN change it.

Harmonizing Your Daily Story

Since you are now the driver of your own bus, I am going to make the assumption that you know what you want out of life and you're making the decision that it is time to create a new bus route. How are you doing? At this moment, are you in analysis paralysis? There are so many new and different things that you wish to try and places you wish to see, what should you do first?

This frequently happens to folks who have been on a bus they haven't been driving for years. You have an overabundance of ideas, am I right?

If that isn't the case, you may have the reverse reaction in which you have drawn a complete blank on the route you wish to take your life. You had what we call a pattern interrupt in your life. You were happily on a bus route of your choosing, and humming along, enjoying the ride, and then all of a sudden life has you on a different bus, going in a totally different direction and you're without a clue on how to proceed with your current route.

Not to worry. No matter what situation you find yourself in, there is a direction for you to drive. Each and every day.

Frequently, I have clients say to me, "Janine, I have no idea what to do." The first thing I recommend to folks who have no idea what to do or have an overabundance of ideas on what to do is this: I respectfully request that you allow yourself three minutes of meditation each morning. Now you may or may not have ever meditated, but you may be thinking that three minutes of meditation has no value to you in this current situation that you find yourself in. You want to ACT; you want to DO something. But as we mentioned before in Chapter 4, there is a difference between motivation and inspiration. And you really want to make sure that you are driving your bus through inspired action. Don't drive when your actions are dictated by fears and insecurities that are phantoms dressed up by your subconscious mind.

By taking the time to meditate each morning and evening, you are allowing yourself to receive the best advice you could ever get, and that is from your Higher Self or your Inner Knowingness. That is the energy you want to tap into for the unvarnished answers. The answers for the life you want to create, not the life that leaves you feeling exhausted, depressed, or unenthused. You want to live a vibrant, thriving, energetic life, right?

The first step is focusing on the experiences you want to have rather than focusing on the experiences you are currently living. Most of the time, we are our own biggest obstacle. So it is up to us to make the changes in ourselves that we wish we could change in others, right? So what type of person do you wish to become? What are the skill sets you want to possess? What are the activities you want to engage in?

Decide on the answers to these questions and then we will move on to changing the way your emotions rule your experiences.

Harmonizing Your Emotional Reactions and Triggers

If you are a human being on planet Earth, you have had joyous experiences and you've had devastating experiences. Welcome to the emotional rollercoaster we call life. Believe it or not, you signed onto this ride because you wanted these rollercoaster experiences. Now, maybe you're ready for a bit more steadiness in your emotional responses to things. Maybe you're ready to have a bit more control over the emotional turmoil you've been feeling as of late. Here is a way for you to start working through the reactions you are having each moment rather than focusing on past or perceived future hurts.

Many times we will create a positive or negative experience because we have judged it to be so. Just because I step onto my bathroom scale and I see that I have gained five pounds doesn't mean this is "bad" and I need to start taking myself to task over what I have eaten over the past few weeks. What is this piece of data in relationship to? The fact that my body changes on an hourly basis depending upon my water intake or the fact that I need to increase my movement time?

We have an inner judge that decides what is right and wrong for us on a minute-by-minute basis. Um, who put that guy in charge? I know I didn't! So, when it comes to harmonizing your head and your heart, it is time to put in charge the woman who nurtures us, comforts us, and brings us peace to our topsy-turvy responses to things. You do this by finding what brings you comfort or joy in each moment. Meditation allows you to open your heart to new possibilities and potentials. Following your joy or your comfort allows you to define more clearly what is good for you.

For years, I've been told that I drink too much coffee. For years, I've seen how my body responds to coffee. I've had times where I didn't drink coffee or have chocolate for six months. I've had times where I ingested an overabundance of caffeine and times where I was caffeine free. The point is this: coffee is calmative for me. It wasn't until 2009 that I ever heard there were some people for which coffee was actually good. The advent of the internet has allowed us more options of living and learning than ever before. Now, it is time for you to focus on your own mind and body to learn what is best for your own homeostasis in your life.

Harmonizing Your Thoughts with Your Highest Good

When it comes to harmonizing your thoughts with your own highest good, the best technique I've ever found was through Eckhart Tolle's "Power of Now," which was his first book. I like the way he describes this sort of thinking better in his later work, "A New Earth." That book really set my mind to work on my thinking of things that were in my highest and best good.

What do I mean by this? If you are focused on the past and you are thinking of things that hurt your heart or caused you to feel awful, why do you stay there? That would be your ego. It wants to keep spinning the tales of things that are trauma and drama because it is bored. When your mind becomes bored, it will try to gain control by thinking of things that are unpleasant, or it will get to work on determining what is the next problem it needs to solve. Basically, the mind wants to do ANYTHING but be bored.

This can cause your heart and your head to go to war. The heart wishes for a peaceful place, a nurturing place, and a place of creativity. It is difficult to be in this place when the mind is busy telling the heart it doesn't have time to be creative. There are BIG problems to solve or there are MORE things to do rather than sit and be creative. It is a way of keeping you from creating the life you want if your mind can get you to focus on things that you:

1. Don't have control over
2. Don't have ready solutions for

By focusing on these sorts of situations, you can get sucked down a rabbit hole of what if's and why me's and should've, could've, and would've. The ego can sit and admire its own handiwork of keeping you churning and burning on problems that don't exist, situations that haven't occurred, and fears that will never manifest, because you're making better decisions than in times past.

To harmonize your head and your heart is not hard work. It is actually the opposite. It is allowing your mind to relax and rest and allowing your heart to sing. I know this may all sound like total nonsense, but it really is as simple as letting the ego know that you will be thinking about what is happening right now and nothing else for the next three minutes. You focus on your breathing and that is it. The ego will get bored and try to derail your focus, but that is not your concern. Your only concern is to focus on the harmony of your breath and then when you feel like it, allow yourself to hum or sing. Make a noise of some kind that is voluntary and through your own creation. By humming or singing, you are creating a tune of your own. Even if it is a tune you've heard before, that doesn't matter. What matters is your creation.

By this simple act of creation, you have harmonized your head and your heart. You focused on your breathing, and you have allowed your heart to sing a song of its own creation, and you've allowed your mind a moment of joy in the creation of its own moment for its own pleasure.

This is self-empowerment.

Harmonizing with Your Community

As you decide on the best way for you to live your life, there are people around you who won't want you to change, and others that will support your change. For those who wish to make changes in their lives, they know how important it is to have people around them that are supportive in the new path they have chosen for themselves.

Realize that as you walk down this new path, you will need to keep a few things in mind:

First, you will need to drop your assumptions about yourself and others. This is a funny one to bring up, but it is important if you are going to move forward. When you think you KNOW how someone is going to react, you don't allow them an opportunity to grow with you.

Second, stay fixated on your target of your journey, no matter what others may say or suggest to you. Unless their advice will allow you to move quicker or less expensively toward your journey, don't alter where you wish to go. Be your own #1 fan. You are your own visionary.

Third, people don't always have the best advice for your life. No matter what path you are walking. It could be a well-worn path, but you know what is best for you, and that is what matters.

Fourth, you are your own best friend. How would you coach your best friend to move into this community with the changes you are making? You give great advice to people. Listen to how you are advising them! Now, take your own advice.

Example: I have been waking up at 3 a.m. for over 14 years as of this writing. When I first started popping awake, I was told a variety of things that were "wrong" with me:

It is probably all that coffee you drink.

You shouldn't eat past 6 p.m.

You aren't exercising enough.

Are you sure you're not premenopausal?

You probably just need to go to bed later.

The list could go on. What I learned was rather than lying in bed thinking something was wrong with me, I got up and read books. When I got tired, I'd go back and lay down and get a few more hours of sleep.

When I first started this process, I was still under the assumption that this was "incorrect" behavior. That this sort of sleeping was "wrong" and that I needed to change something in my life to get back to sleeping in the way I had been taught. Can you imagine? I was holding myself to a model of behavior that no longer worked for my 40-year-old body!

I then started getting up in the middle of the night, and rather than read, I would meditate. I would meditate for hours, then I started to learn that

I actually needed to write books again. I had written books before on debt-free living and wealth accumulation, but now I realized I needed to start writing spiritually-based books.

After that realization, I was off and running. From that day to this, I consistently wake up in the wee hours of the night and realize that I need to be writing, creating, or doing something that is in alignment with my heart. There are times I am making videos, recording an audiobook, or writing an article during my creative time of night. I've learned that as a creator of my own life, I literally have to operate at a different clock time than other humans. Once I started seeing this as my personal brand of "normal," I never looked back with longing for my former sleep schedule.

However, the rest of my family still gives me good -natured humor on the fact that I go to bed by 9 p.m. Yes, I seem to live with a bunch of night owls relative to my schedule. But that is the power of living your own life and creating your own way. I have since taught over 90 online courses, written 12 books, recorded four audiobooks, created four different podcasts with over 300 episodes, all because I allowed myself to sleep on my own timetable. That behavior alone has done more to assist me in living my authentic, harmonious life than any other habit I have created for myself!

CHAPTER #8

LEAVING THE CROSSROADS ON YOUR CREATIVE JOURNEY

It is our hope that by the time you have hit this chapter, you've had some ideas pop into your head on what it is you are to do next in your life. We know that you already have had a few glimmerings that have stirred in your heart, but now it is time for you to move into making a decision one way or another so that you move out of the indecision of standing at the crossroads.

If you feel like you are still stuck in the middle of the crossroads by this point of the book, and you've done your best to answer the questions that Reno and I have posed to you, then we know it doesn't matter what direction you go in.

The point is this: move. Pick. Decide.

You won't pick wrong. You'll start something new and amazing just by making the decision! The decision itself is better than standing at a crossroads and waiting for something to happen. Waiting is only good for so long, but if this book has made its way into your hands, the time of waiting is done. Consider this book a wakeup call to ACT. And ACT now. You are at the chapter where we discuss the journey that you are taking.

Before you step out, there are a few things for you to take along with you. They are reminders to keep your momentum going even if you find yourself stalling out again or at another crossroad down the way.

Sharing Your Story

Learn to share your story carefully. If you are ever asked about your past, be careful of what you share. You want to create a new journey for yourself and your life, not a repeat or a rehash of things that have come before. Often when people ask me about my past, I frequently give them a sentence or two, but more often I speak to them of my current project or my vision for my life in the future. It makes me happy, enthusiastic, and energized to discuss what my current creation is looking like and where I am taking it.

Writing Your Story

This is the most powerful technique I have ever found. Every day I write out what I want my life to look like. I have written my goals, my targets, and my desires for myself and my life for years. I have gone through multiple notebooks as I have written and written and written. Study after study of successful people have shown this is common. The visionaries we admire, the leaders we praise, all had habits that kept their minds and their hearts harmonized: obsessive, consistent habits that were in alignment with their visions.

There are daily habits each leader or visionary had that kept them attuned to where they were going in their lives and kept them focused on their objectives with a zeal that annoyed, frustrated, and exasperated those around them. But in the end, you can't help but admire their results. So, when it comes to what you want in your life, I recommend you start writing down your desires. To begin with, write down what the end result looks like.

Example:

Instead of writing down "I want to weigh 145 pounds" when you weigh 167 pounds, I would write... "I am thankful for the body I have and the strength that comes to me each day."

In my own life I write some of the following each day:

I am thankful for who I am.

I am thankful for how I feel right now.

I am thankful for this point in my life.

I am thankful that my inner being is aware of me.

I feel happy that there is nothing I'd rather do than be me.

This is a delicious life I am living.

I'm excited by what is going to unfold.

I'm excited by the possibilities and the potentials.

I love the feeling of my intention and intuitiveness.

I love the feeling of receiving and alignment.

I adore the trust people have in me.

I love the feeling of right place and right time.

I am thankful for my thriving life.

I am thankful for the people and the relationships in my life.

Now, you may wish to write down different statements. The whole point is to write down the generic things that make you feel good right now. I ended up amalgamating these statements over a period of years and have realized that my life and my joy is boiled down to these essential elements. Your essential elements will be different. Start with something, and as you move through your daily writing of statements, your heart will lead you to write more and more positive comments that work best for you and your life situation.

Creating Your Message

"Have you thought about writing a book?" I have been asked this question most of my life. People loved the stories I shared and they frequently mentioned I needed to write a book. Now that I have written books, I have people suggest different things I could do to share my story. To give you an idea on the evolution of storytelling in our world:

In 1996, "Have you ever considered teaching?"

In 2002, "Have you written a book?"

In 2004, " Have you ever considered blogging?"

In 2015, "Why don't you do a podcast on this subject?"

In 2018, "Have you considered getting syndicated on radio?"

In 2019, "Do you have your own channel on YouTube?"

That gives you an idea on how much things have changed and the different ways that you can share your message. The point of having a message to share is this:

You are a creative force in this world. How do you wish to share what you know?

Joining a Community of Likeminded Folks

Last but not least is joining a community. It is so easy to do these days and it is important for you to not be discouraged as you look for a group of people of like mind. There are more groups, clubs, activities, and communities that you can be a part of than ever before. That also brings with it a unique set of challenges. Be sure to establish the qualifications you need to have in place before you align yourself with anyone or any group.

First off, it is important that you know what you are looking for from the community. Are you there to be a participant in the activities? Do you wish to lead? Do you wish to have support? Maybe you are looking for accountability? Define what it is you are looking for first. Then seek it out.

Yes, this may seem like an obvious step, but I specialize in the obvious. I mention the obvious a lot: why? Because too many people take the obvious in life for granted. I want you to find the gold in your own life first before you go seeking it elsewhere. It will save you a lot of time, resources, and heartache.

We all need community at some point. If for nothing else, then to give us an opportunity to break out of our own thoughts, right?

Second, decide what you are willing to give to the community. This will allow you the opportunity to say "no" before you overcommit yourself or take on a project that is not in alignment with your message. Most communities have no difficulty with you being a "part" of them for over a year before committing to an activity. Give yourself permission to ride along for a bit to see if the group dynamic is what you are desiring for yourself.

Lastly, by clearly knowing what you want to ask of the group and what you are willing to give to the group, it becomes quite easy and simple to share yourself with the group because there is no fear of being "taken advantage of" nor of "giving too much for no return!" By taking the time to define these two factors, you'll stay in alignment with your ability to be yourself while sharing what you have with others. Well done!

Becoming an Eagle

In 2017, two-wheel walkers were placed side-by-side at a metaphysical fair. At first, Reno and I had no idea why we had been placed next to one another by the event's organizer. It seemed like the worst thing that could have happened. As each of us set about our tasks of assisting the people who came to us, we spoke between our sessions and shared our experiences with one another. We quickly learned the value of that chance meeting. The perspectives we brought to each subject as well as the mindset we shared brought clarity and details to our discussions.

It wasn't long until we started doing Crow Lodges and Women's Retreats for our communities together. For years we worked with people individually as well as a team. We referred clients to one another and shared our knowledge and workings at fairs all over Colorado and Wyoming. It is a friendship that has borne good fruit over and over again.

We now encourage you, dear reader, to do the same. Take those moments that may have seemed like the worst things that have happened to you and reframe them into answering this statement.

How was that a good thing for me?

When you ask your brain to solve that sort of a problem, you take the frequency of the event and rather than seeing it in a dark or negative perspective, you bring up the frequency of the memory into a more positive experience. Recently, I had a betrayal from a dear friend of over 50 years. I was stunned, shocked, and unable to process the event for the first few weeks. I sought counseling and, after eight months, stumbled upon the question above as a technique. It was a YouTube video made by a 30-year -old artist who had suffered sexual abuse as a young boy and had retreated into the world of drugs and alcoholism. He had managed to pull himself out of that dark place through his art and a supportive community of friends. Through his journey, he had created these videos to assist other people with their mental health paths.

It was through this young man that I realized I needed to reframe this friend's betrayal into "an experience I had with a friend." I immediately began to feel better. That was a great sign! I continually worked on all the ways that this experience was good for me. I started writing out lists of things that were good about it and I began to feel better and better and better. Rather than being in that dark, depressed, and horrid emotional cage, I felt freed and able to move forward with my relationships. Now, four years later, I had a two-hour phone call recently with this person, and I was healed of my emotional issues surrounding this experience. I realized through this experience that how I view the world and the people in it can be built into a fun-filled adventure, or I could make it into a hellish prison of trauma and abuse, all by my own attitude and expectations.

Reno and I wish for you to be able to take your personal life and make it heaven on earth. Even if you only experience such joy and peace during certain moments of the day, that is better than never feeling those moments. You are a light-bringer on this planet. It is up to you to share with others the beauty that you see in your life. The joy that you feel and the delight that you experience at seeing the first butterfly of spring. You bring a powerful and wondrous perspective to this planet. Thank you for being here and thank you for sharing what you know with Reno and I and our community.

We encourage you to share what you know with us. To teach us what you have learned through your gifts as well as allow us to share with you what we have learned through the working of our gifts.

It is through this sort of collaboration that we can expand our influence and make our parts of the world a better place.

Reno and I love meeting mystics from all over the world. No matter if you are just learning to use your Reiki skills, or if you are a seasoned healer and have been a mystic since you hit the planet, we would enjoy being able to get to know you better and incorporate your perspective into our community and ceremonies.

CHAPTER 9

NEXT STEPS: THE PRACTICAL MYSTICS COMMUNITY

One of the joys of being a part of the Practical Mystics Community is having a place to meet on Zoom where you can be with people of like mind and enjoy the 90 minutes of time with them, either learning something new or sharing a part of what is going on in your region of the world.

This is where you get to meet new folks as well as learn that you are not alone in your gifts or abilities. This is a place where you can bring your challenges or speed bumps and see how others have handled similar situations in their lives.

The Practical Mystics meet once a month, and you can sign up for free by visiting us here: https://thepracticalmystics.com/monthlymeetings

Reno and I hold retreats for women throughout the year.

Three of our quarterly retreats are held online, and then once a year we have in-person retreats during the month of June in Colorado.

We offer Monthly Programs & Workshops for those who wish to expand their knowledge with their own skill sets.

Lastly, there is our Wheel Walkers training & certification program. You are welcome to apply, but we encourage you to visit us during our free monthly meetings first.

ABOUT RENO LONGMOONS

Reno has a lifetime of experience with over 40 years as an Energy Worker. Her wisdom brings comfort to her clients in all services that she offers. Blessed with many gifts by Spirit, Reno is able to invigorate positive energy within a home to communicate and cleanse any imprinted energy or outside energies within your space(s).

Clients describe working with Reno as feeling immediately safe and within a trusted space as she guides them through these special ceremonies:

Wheel Walking – a tool to connect with Spirit for guidance and understating. Workshops designed to teach you this method for your personal growth and relationship with the Creator.

Symbol Reading – interactive intuitive reading between Spirit, you, and Reno.

Life Coaching Sessions – based on the principals of the Toltec. A guide to inner wisdom and self-reliance. You may learn more about her on her website: https://www.hollowboneartistry.com.

ABOUT JANINE BOLON

Janine "Dancing Crow" Bolon is a Sacred Clown, Shaman, Bell Dancer, and First Chakra Healer. After 20+ years of working with an enlightened Hindu Guru and the Native American Grandmothers and Grandfathers, she was initiated into the ThunderClan after being struck by lightning.

Bring your intentions for the life changes you wish to create for yourself, and she will work with you using a variety of techniques to guide you in creating the lifestyle you desire.

Janine's specialty is integrating high frequency spirituality into grounded daily living (such as having money to do the stuff you want to do.)

Learn more about her community here: https://thepracticalmystics.com.

ANNOTATED BIBLIOGRAPHY

These are some books that have helped Reno and I along our journey. These resources will not replace meditation for developing your connection with your Higher Self, but they offer reassurance that you are not alone on your path. Many types of mystics have been successful at self-discovery, even in the face of major challenges. These are the inspirational books that have helped us continue expanding our gifts and talents even when we wanted to hide from life.

Reno's Recommendations:

The 4 Agreements, Don Miguel Ruiz. This book is what I recommend to all mystics that wish to build a community of any kind. Whether it is online, in person, or retreats. When you get ready to move out into the world and organize people for a group enterprise, The 4 Agreements is a great foundation to maintain participants' understanding of what we expect from them and what they can expect from us as facilitators.

Jumping Mouse: A Story about Inner Trust, Mary Elizabeth Marlow. I think I've already explained quite clearly the profound effect of Jumping Mouse in my life. All I wish to share with you today is an invitation to read this amazing story and then adapt its promptings into your own life story.

Janine's Recommendations:

Ask and It is Given, Esther and Jerry Hicks. If you enjoy a book that teaches and then gives you honest-to-goodness practice steps, this is for you. When I read this book in 2015, I loved how the exercises walked me through different types of systems for thinking through my self-limiting beliefs and emotions. There are over 22 different systems to choose from for making your life better. This is my go -to book for emotional speed bumps.

Autobiography of a Yogi, Paramahansa Yogananda. This landmark book got me into a spiritual form of discipline that would last the rest of my life. Not everyone is as single-minded as I am when it comes to goal-setting, but Yogananda's experiences with his awakening are eloquently described, giving you another example of what it means to engage in life and still keep a quietness of mind amidst chaos.

How We Die: Reflections on Life's Final chapter, Sherwin B. Nuland. I read this book in 1995 when I was doing a lot of coaching and going through grief. It was a great reminder that we will all die and it is up to us to figure out what our death should look like. After considering the way my mom died in 1987, I was better able to make choices on how I wanted to die after reading this book. The latest edition has an added chapter on the current practices in healthcare and ways that you might want your family to work with you should you develop a terminal illness, or one of the seven major diseases that can be terminal. Yes, the book was written 20 years ago, but not much has changed in the process of dying: only the amount of control patients now have in their care.

The Power of Myth, Joseph Campbell. Campbell experienced enlightenment at the age of 27 and spent the rest of his life using academic scholarship and lectures to teach what he knew. He was brilliant at integrating the stories and legends of tribal peoples all over the world and using their metaphors to create purposeful stories for his readers, students, and community. This book helped me incorporate the Greek, Roman, and Hindu perspectives into my Christian metaphors as I moved along my spiritual journey. Campbell also helped me overcome the frustrations of fitting language to transcendent experiences.

The New Earth, Eckhart Tolle. For those that struggle with wayward thoughts and challenging mental trash talk, you will love how Tolle works with people and shares with them how to get out of their own way. He offers excellent tips and techniques that assist you in giving up the concept that "You are your Mind." He proves to you step-by-step that you are not your thoughts. I've read this book more in its audio-book form rather than its written word form to much success. Frequently, I go to sleep listening to Tolle's voice sharing his methods and personal journey. No matter what format you choose to use with this book, you'll find comfort with the information shared by Tolle.

PERSONAL NOTES

(I write in books when I read them, I wanted you to have
some pages to record your thoughts too!)

CREATING WITH THE DIVINE

★ ★ ★ ★ ★

WELCOME & THANK YOU!

This multi-media book entitles you to a special gift that is the perfect companion to *Creating with the Divine*.

It is a group of videos that assist with meditation, expansion of your personal skills as well as a checklist to see what skills you may already possess and which ones you may be ready to improve.

This collection of media will allow you to study and improve your own metaphysical gifts in greater detail!

DOWNLOAD TODAY!

ThePracticalMystics.com/thanks

★ ★ ★ ★ ★

www.ingramcontent.com/pod-product-compliance
Lightning Source LLC
Chambersburg PA
CBHW071816020426
42331CB00007B/1505